BEST FRIENDS
FOR FRANCES

by RUSSELL HOBAN
Pictures by LILLIAN HOBAN

HARPER & ROW, PUBLISHERS

New York, Evanston, and London

For Frances's friends everywhere

It was a pleasant summer morning,
so Frances took her bat and her ball
and some chocolate sandwich cookies and went outside.
"Will you play ball with me?" Frances's little sister
Gloria called to her as she was leaving.
"No," said Frances. "You are too little."
Gloria sat down on the back steps and cried.
Frances walked over to her friend Albert's house,
singing a little song:

> *Sisters that are much too small*
> *To throw or catch or bat a ball*
> *Are really not much good at all,*
> *Except for crying.*

When Frances got to Albert's house,
he was just coming out, and he was carrying
a large, heavy-looking brown paper bag.
"Let's play baseball," said Frances.
"I can't," said Albert. "Today is my wandering day."
"Where do you wander?" said Frances.
"I don't know," said Albert. "I just go around
until I get hungry, and then I eat my lunch."
"That looks like a big lunch," said Frances.
"It's nothing much," said Albert. "Four or five

sandwiches and some apples and bananas
and two packages of cupcakes
and a quart of chocolate milk."
"Can I wander with you?" asked Frances.
"I only have one lunch," said Albert.
"I'll bring my own," said Frances.
"I'll run home and get it right away."
"No," said Albert, "I think I better go by myself.
The things I do on my wandering days
aren't things you can do."

"Like what?" said Frances.

"Catching snakes," said Albert. "Throwing stones at telephone poles. A little frog work maybe. Walking on fences. Whistling with grass blades. Looking for crow feathers."

"I can do all that," said Frances, "except for the frog work and the snakes."

"That's what I mean," said Albert.

"I'd have to ruin the whole day, showing you how. I'll see you tomorrow."

Then Albert went off to wander, and Frances walked slowly home with her bat and ball, singing:

Fat boys that eat too much lunch
Can't do a thing but munch and crunch
And play with snakes and frogs.

When Frances got home, Gloria said,
"Will you play ball with me now?"

"You can't bat and you can't catch," said Frances,
"and you can't throw either."

"I can if you stand close," said Gloria.

"All right," said Frances,
and she played ball with Gloria.

9

The next morning when Frances went to Albert's house,
Albert was playing ball with his friend Harold.
"Can I play?" asked Frances.
"She's not much good," said Harold to Albert,
"and besides, this is a no-girls game."
"Can't I play?" said Frances to Albert.
"Well, it *is* a no-girls game," said Albert.

"All right," said Frances. "Then I will go home
and play a no-boys game with my sister Gloria,
Mr. Fat Albert. So ha, ha, ha."
Frances walked home, and as she walked she sang:

Boys to throw and catch and bat
Are all the friends that Mr. Fat
Albert will have from now on.
He will not have me.

When Frances got home, Gloria said,
"How did you play so fast that you are home so soon?"
"It was a fast game," said Frances.
"You're lucky that you have a friend to play with,"
said Gloria. "I wish I had a friend."

"I thought Ida was your friend," said Frances.
"Ida is away at camp," said Gloria,
"and when she is here she only wants to play
dolls or tea party. She never wants
to catch frogs or play ball."
"Can you catch frogs?" asked Frances.
"I use Father's old hat," said Gloria.
"Shall I show you how?"
"Later," said Frances. "Do you want to play ball?"
"All right," said Gloria.
"If any boys come, they can't play," said Frances,
"and I think I will be your friend now."
"How can a sister be a friend?" said Gloria.
"You'll see," said Frances.
"For frogs and ball *and* tea parties and dolls?"
said Gloria.
"Yes," said Frances.

"And will you show me how to print my name?"
said Gloria, "And tell me what the letters and numbers
say when I make letters and numbers?"
"Yes," said Frances.
"Then you will be my best friend," said Gloria.
"Will it be just today, or longer?"
"Longer," said Frances. "And today we are going to do
something big, with no boys."
"What?" said Gloria.
"We will have an outing," said Frances,
"and there will be a picnic and songs
and games and prizes."
Mother helped Frances and Gloria get everything ready
and packed in Frances's wagon.

16

Then Frances and Gloria went off to the outing.
In the wagon was a picnic lunch in a hamper.
There were also two burlap sacks for the sack race,
an egg for the egg toss, and a jar with two frogs in it
that Gloria had caught for the frog-jumping contest.
And there were balloons and lollipops for prizes.
Frances had made a sign to carry on the outing too.
It said:

BEST FRIENDS

OUTING

NO BOYS

Frances and Gloria held the sign high
as they passed Albert's house, and Frances sang:

When best friends have an outing,
There are jolly times in store.
There are games and there are prizes,
There is also something more.
There is something in a hamper
That is very good to eat.
When best friends have an outing,
It's a very special treat,
With no boys.

"What is in that hamper?" asked Albert
as he came running out of his house.
"I don't know," said Frances. "Nothing much.
Hard-boiled eggs and whole fresh tomatoes.
Carrot and celery sticks. There are some
cream cheese-and-chives sandwiches, I think,
and cream cheese-and-jelly sandwiches too,
and salami-and-egg and pepper-and-egg sandwiches.
Cole slaw and potato chips, of course.
Ice-cold root beer packed in ice,
and watermelon and strawberries and cream for dessert.

And there are other things I forget,
like black and green olives and pickles and popsicles
and probably some pretzels and things like that.
And there are salt and pepper shakers and napkins
and a checked tablecloth,
which is the way girls do it."
"Could I come along on the eating?" said Albert.
"You mean outing," said Frances.
"Outing, I mean," said Albert. "Could I come along?
That wagon looks very heavy to pull,
and you will probably get all tired out unless I help you."
"I don't know," said Frances.
"You can see from the sign that this is a no-boys outing
and it is only for best friends."
"What good is an outing without boys?" said Albert.
"It is just as good as a ball game without girls,"
said Frances, "and maybe a whole lot better."
"Can't I be a best friend?" asked Albert.
"I don't think it is the kind of thing you can do,"
said Frances, "and it would ruin my whole day
to have to explain it to you."

"I can do it," said Gloria.

"I can be a best friend, and I can catch frogs too."

"I can catch frogs *and* snakes," said Albert.

"Let him be a best friend," said Gloria,

"and he can show me how to catch snakes."

"I'll get my snake pillowcase right now," said Albert.

"Well, I'm not sure," said Frances. "Maybe you'll be best friends when it is goodies-in-the-hamper time, but how about when it is no-girls-baseball time?"

"When we are best friends, there won't be
any no-girls baseball," said Albert.
"All right," said Frances, and she crossed out
the NO BOYS on the sign.
Then they started off again. Albert pulled the wagon
to the outing place while Frances and Gloria
walked ahead with the sign.

The outing place was at the maple tree on the hill
by the pond. Everybody had a good time there.
First, Albert caught a snake for Gloria,
and then they played games.
Gloria won the sack race, Frances won the egg toss,
and Albert won the frog-jumping contest
with a fresh frog he caught right there at the pond.
So everybody won a prize. Then Frances
made up a party song, and everybody sang it:

When the wasps and the bumblebees have a party,
Nobody comes that can't buzz.
When the chicks and the ducklings have an outing,
Everyone has to wear fuzz.
When the frog and the snake
Have their yearly clambake,
There's plenty of wiggling and hopping.
They splash in the pond
And the marshes beyond,
And everyone has to get sopping.

"And at the Best Friends' Outing," said Albert,
"everyone has to eat, don't they?"
"Yes," said Frances and Gloria, and they opened the hamper.
"Maybe we packed too much," said Frances.
"I'm not sure we can eat it all."
"That is what best friends are for," said Albert
as he quickly spread the tablecloth.
"I will help you finish it all."

That is what Albert did, and when the picnic was over,
the hamper was not heavy at all.

"I call that a good outing," said Albert.
And he gave Frances and Gloria a ride in the wagon
while he pulled it all the way home.

The next morning Albert came over
with a bunch of daisies for Frances.
"What are the daisies for?" said Frances.
"Well," said Albert, "we are best friends now,
and I am a boy. So that makes me your best boyfriend,
and that is why I brought you the daisies."
"Thank you," said Frances.
Then Gloria sat down on the steps and cried.
"Why are you crying?" said Frances.

"Because now you have Albert to be your best boyfriend and bring you flowers and play ball with," said Gloria, "and you won't be my best friend anymore."
"Yes, I will," said Frances. "And besides, I am not sure that I am going to let Albert be my boyfriend."
"Then let him be mine," said Gloria.
"Not so fast," said Frances. "It was only yesterday that you got to be big enough to play baseball.
But I will give you half the daisies Albert gave me."
So Frances gave Gloria half the daisies, and Gloria stopped crying.
Then Harold came over, and everybody played baseball—Gloria too.